Well Since You Asked

Toni Lynn

BookLeaf Publishing

Presentation by *BookLeaf Publishing*

Web: www.bookleafpub.com

E-mail: info@bookleafpub.com

ISBN: 978-93-95784-04-7

First edition 2022

DEDICATION

To the one who made me feel there was a reason to keep living and loving. And to my Superman who is no longer with us.

ACKNOWLEDGEMENT

Thank you to all of those who have supported me, believed in me and encouraged me. Who listened to me talk about writing and pushed me to write when I kept saying there was no reason to write. I love you all.

Wrong Generation

I'm in the wrong generation
The wrong time period
The wrong era.
This time I'm in, isn't a good fit for me
For my beliefs, desires, wants or needs
Feels like a pair of ill-fitting pants
Uncomfortable as hell and not even cute
Love, intimacy, loyalty, devotion
These are what my spirit craves
Dates, conversations, energy vibes
This is what my soul desires
Honor, trust, admiration, respect
This is what my emotional mind wants
Cuddles, soft kisses, love taps, hugs
This is what my body wishes for

But this time I'm in now, this era
They want booty calls and wyd texts
Always looking for their next conquest
Quick to throw in the towel, walk away
Whenever a sliver of feeling arises
No commitment yet they feel entitled to it
Stunting for social media, aching for a like
Virtually cheating through pictures
Unashamedly flirting in every inbox

Yea this time I'm in, not the best fit
Feel like the new kid in town
Standing still looking around
This era I'm in its soul depressing

Changing the narrative

I am damaged
I am broken
I am divorced
I am tatted
I am overweight
I am depressed
I am not enough
Not good enough
Not pretty enough
Not smart enough
Not motivated enough
Not aggressive enough
Yet honestly, these are not my truths.
These may be my inner critic
The inner voice telling me my negatives
And man does that voice get loud
But now it's time to quite the ruckus
Speak life into myself, uplift myself
Encourage and strengthen myself
Because how can anyone love me
Before I've successfully loved me
How can anyone pour into me
When I am busy knocking holes in my vessel
I am mosaic art, beautifully broken but excellent
craftsmanship in recreating what's seen

Friends and family, the grout that helps me put
my pieces together.
I am valued and valuable.
Unwilling to settle in any situation
I am a walking art piece.
Beautifully telling my story through each tattoo
I am full of love waiting to be shared
Overflowing with goodness, joy, hope teeming
over with romance
It's time to change the narrative of who I am.

Can you handle it?

Can you handle it?
Not my body that I see you admire
Not the thickness of my thighs you imagine
wrapped around you
Or the weight of my ass you imagine palming
Or the softness of my breast that you imagine
kissing.
I'm challenging you to handle more.

Can you handle it?
My mind. My personality. My attitude.
The trinity locked inside this body you undress
with your eyes.
The thoughts that I have and speak with
confidence.
The persona that comes forth depending on my
situation.
The mood that could greet you depending on
your actions.
I'm challenging you too more.

Can you handle it?
See if the focus is only physical then you'll be
disappointed.
Cuz the delivery won't match the package.
If my body is all you see and desire, there's
websites that can take you higher.
I'm challenging you to handle more.

Can you handle it?
My connection is no longer just physical.
I don't reach my point if that's all there is.
I've gotten to that moment where the trinity are
no longer willing to hide.
They've done an override on the system and are
demanding more.
So, before you open this door just know
I'm challenging you to handle more

Desire vs Wants

Flowers, cards, candy
Good morning and good night messages
Laid on the couch watching nothing
Simply enjoying each other's presence
Random date nights, spontaneous link ups
Sensual massages to release the tension
Of the days stress.
What I desire.

Booty call messages and random pics
Innuendos of positions you'd like me in
Hints at a threesome,
Pondering on my oral skills
Wondering what pleasures I can bring you
Not caring about mine
What I receive

What I wish for and want versus what I
constantly receive
Starkly different to the point of depression
And when I say no thanks
Now I'm a bitch, whore, ugly, and no good
When in the initial contact
I was sweetie, baby, beautiful

I guess the fact that I'm not willing to drop to
my knees
And bless your "lil man"
Not willing to take in your essence
Changes my standings in your eyes
For the life of me I can never understand
What lead you to believe that
Drinking from your fountain
Is what I even desired
When we both know I deserve more.

What is this?

Is this it? Have I found love?
Have I found the One?
The one that makes me want to take that road
Throw out the numbers in my phone
Turn in my playa card
And let him hold my heart

Is this it? Have I found love?
The one where it's beyond the physical
Tapping into the mental and spiritual
Cuz can't lie, my body says yeah
But my heart says wait. Stay on hold
Scared and not wanting to be left out in the cold.

Is this it? Have I found love?
The one who respects me
Honors and cherishes me
Comforts, humors, and uplifts me
The one who sees me for me
And wants me but is willing to work for me

Is this it? Have I found love?
Have I found the One
The One G-d wants for me
The One G-d created to hold me
Comforting me when I need that physical touch
The One G-d wants to talk to me and with me
When I am in need of that physical voice

Is this it? Have I found love?
Have I found the One?
I think that I have, and I am getting lost in this
thought
And man-Love feels good

Be

Be careful I'm fragile
I might come off as tough
Looking like I got it all
And everything is together
But looks are deceiving
And inside it looks like a hurricane town

Be careful I'm cautious
I want a relationship
But can't just leap into it
My heart and my trust
Those are my biggest gifts
And for me to give them
Means I want a lifetime love

Be careful I'm scarred
Not by physical abuse
But mental and emotional
And these scars are still fresh
Years don't heal them fast
And small things can reopen them

So be careful with me
Be gentle and kind
Be understanding and compassionate

Be patient and attentive
But most of all caring
Because I am willing to give myself to you
If you will just Be

Wondering

Would you still consider me, if you really knew
me
If you really knew my past, hell even my present
Would I still be a Queen if you could really see
the scars
The things that I have done I don't regret
But some of them I guess I would change

I am far from perfect, not even close to great
The things I have done would make some look
at me different
I could pass the blame on who made me this
way
But at the end of it all I made most of the
choices on my own

I mean, the blame could go to the high school
senior
Who saw the new freshman as another notch to
add to his belt
And even though I held out
Ignored the pressure and advances
The rumors still spread though
Without many knowing the full truth
All that senior did was kiss my valley

Or maybe, the blame lies with the childhood
friend
Who called me his sister in public
But treated me as his lover in the dark
Watching him date and love others
While ignoring me in that aspect, never given a
chance
Calling on me only when the need to be physical
arose
Confiding in me with his secrets and pains
Sharing with me his dreams
Allowing me to see his vulnerability
But only behind closed doors

But in all honesty the blame lies within me
For always wanting to see the good in others
Even when their ugly sides are staring me in the
face
Believing that I meant more to them
Over playing my role in their lives

So, knowing all this
Would you still consider me?

Ready

Is she ready for you? Are you ready for her?
Did I prepare you properly enough to fully
Love her, appreciate her, enjoy her, desire her
Is my time with you complete?
Can I store you in my past memories?
Locked away with the others
The ones I've loved and desired
While preparing them for their true HER

See that's my power. My position in life
Very simply-my pain
To dedicate myself to one
Only to watch him choose another over me
I've done much soul searching to figure out
Understand why this is the way it is.

Stayed single and denied my flesh
Trying to have a clear mind to hash this out
And still no clear answer I find
No fault I can seem to fix.

Did I love too hard? Love too much?
Desire too much? Encourage, uplift, support too
much?

Did I simply do too much of whatever?
See baby, you're with me now and its fun
It's great, hell it's a blast
But the distance is starting
The texts are shorter. The visits are less.
And even when you are here with me
Physically and mentally, you are miles away

So, I'm sorry that I don't text first
Sorry that I don't initiate contact
But I know that my time is almost up
And I don't want to impose on her space
 I swallow my hurt and pain
Taking pride in a job I truly never wanted
And all I hope is that
She's ready for you
Because I know
You're ready for her

Us

She's with you
He's with me
Vibing together
Happy in lust
But when things go wrong
She's alone
And he's at home
But we're together
Being for each other
What they aren't for us

Back and forth we go
Careful not to get attached
Cautious not to hurt them
They're innocent in all of this
Not knowing of this bond
This unexplainable hold we have
When it comes to us

We've played this game
Getting better each year
Growing older. Maybe wiser
Each time we're apart
We learn new skills

That we share with each other
The next time we meet

This is the beauty and curse
The good and the bad
of us being Us

Words

You said I love you
And with the same mouth you flirted with
someone else
You said I love you
And with the same mouth you promised
someone else forever
You said I love you
And with the same mouth tore me down for not
catering to you every second of the day
You said I love you
And with the same mouth you later told me you
never wanted me
You said I love you
And with the same mouth proceeded to tell me
how loose I appeared for having friends.
You said I love you
And with the same mouth told me you wanted
me while simultaneously ignoring me

At this point words don't mean shit to me
They're easy for people to use
Throwing them around like an idiot trying to
appear smart
Being used out of context
Or with no functional action to back them up

Just empty promises and watered-down dreams
Sadly, I swallow the bullshit like a thirsty person
needing to be quenched
So, who's really at fault?
You for lying
Or me for believing

Innocent

It started off so innocent
A conscious decision to be friends
Nothing more and nothing less
But that still couldn't hide
The underlying desire and attraction

We tried to keep it buried, hidden
A quick shy glance
A smooth sly touch
Creating a heat sure to burn
Group hangouts turned into just us sessions
Movies and conversations, nothing serious

But in an unexpected moment
Walls came down and the truth was free
A tentative kiss followed by the buried passion
And that earlier decision
That shallow lie of "friends" was consumed
And desire was established

Before we knew, we were meeting secretly
Sharing more than a conversation with each
other
Walking that line between lovers and friends
Becoming the safe space in each other
While publicly pretending there was nothing
there

But remember, it started off so innocent.

Pride

Pride is a hell of a drug
I overdose on that mess daily
Getting a high from the acting
Pretending that nothing bothers me
And I miss no one. Not a single soul
Using the high from pride
To hide the truth for awhile
You see, the thing about pride
It helps mask the hurt and pain
The feeling of rejection and dejection

But the high from pride
Is extremely deceptive and destructive
Causing me to miss out on life
Miss out on love. Miss out on you
Have me not wanting to do things
Make that call. Make that first move
Just stuck watching life go on
Shrugging my shoulders
Nonchalantly saying that's life
Sitting back in the darkness
Letting it cloak me like the perfect coat
Getting another does of the drug called
PRIDE

Scream

I want to scream
I want to throw things
Hear the satisfying sound of broken glass
There's a feeling inside of me
I can't name it. Can't label it
But I feel overwhelmed
Anxiety is my new constant friend
Arms wrapped tight around my chest
Each breath I take feels like a chore
Sleep is fleeting. Barely staying long
Few hours here. Stray hours there
I feel out of control
Of my mind, body, emotions

I want to scream
I want to punch something
Visualizing channeling my anger into that punch
Putting all my anger into that movement
Feeling the satisfaction of the sound
Pleasure in hearing the noise that hit will make
Knowing that if I scream
The sheer pain behind it will rob my voice
Leaving nothing behind but a raspy shadow
A sound no one will listen to

I need to scream
To release this pain
This anger
This hatred.
Because I know if I verbalize it
I will cause more fallout then necessary
Hurting others who really do not deserve that
pain level

I will scream
I will shout it out
I will release
And once done
I will take a deep breath
And focus back on the task at hand.

Prove me Wrong

I wanted you to prove me wrong
To prove to me that my darkest thoughts
Were playing tricks on me
I needed you to prove me wrong
To show me that the world in my head
Was false and incorrect
I asked that you convince me
Without a doubt that I mattered
Instead, you went on about business
Continuing as usual, no changes
Broke my heart with the verbal news
That I wasn't enough
Claimed you still wanted me
But once you walked out my door
I guess that desire fled your thoughts
Now I'm sitting here wondering, again
Why no will fight for me
Why no one wants me in their life
Why am I only good for sex
But not for love

Thank you for proving me right

Anguish

Tonight, the tears finally came
Deep soul weeping escaped my body
Hurt, pain, weariness, and pure exhaustion
All came to a head
The images on the news seared into my brain
Mothers crying, fathers angry, children scared
This is not the normal we were looking for
But years of injustice. Decades of being treated
less than
Less than human
Less than a person
Less than a whole
Centuries of being judged by a color G-d chose
for us.
That all erupted into smashed windows
Busted storefronts
Fire set to squad cars
Watching this play out
With no director yelling Cut
No stunt doubles waiting for their cue
This was a movie playing in real time
As the world raged, the tears finally fell
Tears I've been feeling for days, weeks
Tears that couldn't seem to fall
Fell quickly with ease.

Drenching my face
My voice crying out Lord your people need you
Lord your people are hurting
The words I couldn't form before
Coming out. Faster than my mouth can move
The words came. And the tears fell.
Finally

Shattered

My pieces were shattered
Laying on the ground in a million parts
Some too sharp to attempt to touch
Some so broken, resembling shards of glass
For years I tried to glue them together
But each life event, each change
Broke me again. Leaving more pieces in the
wreckage

So, I stopped trying to fix me
Accepting that the person I was
Could no longer exist
Instead, I began working with the pieces
Leaving on the floor the parts that no longer
were needed
No longer using pointless tactics as my crutch
Learning to love who I was becoming
Instead of yearning for who I use to be
Speaking kindness to myself
Instead of waiting for others to do so

Slowing becoming whole

Forever

I see forever in your eyes
When I look at you
I can bring you up in my mindeye
Without having to find a picture of you
A part of me is anxiously waiting
For the panic and the anxiety of forever
To set in. to come visit
But the truth of the matter is
They won't come. Not today. Not tomorrow
Without realizing it and without trying
I found my person and my peace
In the soul that rests within you
You speak to the innermost part of me
A part no one has ever been able to reach
You see the me no one else chooses to see

G-d

My relationship with G-d is supposed to be a
public display
Something that I am expected to share with
everyone daily
This relationship with an invisible being
But if I am in a relationship with someone of the
same sex
Or sleeping with someone in general
That has to be hidden and shamed.
A person that is physically here in the flesh

G-d knows my heart and knows what's best for
me
My relationship with Him should be personal
However, it is also open to interpretation by
outsiders
Those who feel my relationship with Him needs
adjusting
Because I am not relating the way they would
want me to

It continues to amaze me how many people
Believe they are justified in setting the terms
Putting the boundaries on my relationship with
G-d

How many people believe they are the expert on
being with Him
When they struggle in their own physical
relationships
In church falling out praising Him
But in the streets cussing at people who get in
your way

G-d knows my heart, right?
So, He knows my actions and thoughts.
He knows me in way no human will ever know
me
But me knowing this is still wrong
Because my outward display of love to Him
Does not match your imagination of what love
to Him should look like

You read the word as data, I read it as data
And because of this you feel you are better
inclined to decipher the Bible
My interpretation of His word in my life doesn't
match your blueprint
So, it must be wrong.
But I thought my relationship with G-d was
mine?

Night thoughts

At night when I'm alone
When there's no one but me and myself
That's the hardest and darkest times ever
That time where it's just me and my imagination
The thoughts I hear. the words that are said
I curl in a ball finding strange comfort in the
pain

"You're no good for anyone"
"He never wanted you for anything but sex"
"You know you're not the only one"
"No one will ever love you"
"You're not pretty at all"

An endless litany of faults
Tears washing down my face
The smile I've put in place all day
Long gone and forgotten

"She was better than you"
"You're too much...of something"
"No one wants damaged goods"
"You're too broken to be any good"
"You're never enough"

These are the thoughts that end my day
Try as I may to ignore or change them
Can't silence them or forget them
So I cry my tears while curled up
Taking the words like body blows
Until the sun rises on a new day
That is when
I put my smile in place and laugh
Because I survived my thoughts another night

"You're beautiful and desired"
"You are someone's good thing"
"You are just enough for the one for you"
"The love you desire is out there and does exist"

These words replace the sadness
The unrelenting darkness holding its line
Waiting for the sun to set
The lights to go off and the smile removed
Replacing my Joy with "Truths"

By who's measurement though

I won't measure up
I'll always fall short of some invisible mark
I ill never be the perfect image
That I or you have created in your mind

All I can continue to be is me
Flawed, imperfect, with mistakes and
shortcomings
But the catch is, I love with my all
My heart, my soul, my mind and my body
All that I am is poured into the one
I deem worthy of having me and my attention
I hold nothing back. Lay it all on the table
Take it or leave it.

I don't know any other way to be
And this has cost me every single time
I give my all and get nothing back in return
Unless you count heartbreak, disappointment
and sadness

Leaves me wondering when I will ever be
enough
Good enough, pretty enough, smart enough,
loving enough
Maybe the reality is simply
We all measure life differently

My Love Poem

Billions of people in this world
Millions of mistakes have been made
Thousands of options presented in life
Hundreds of decisions to make
Tens of profiles to view
Yet you're the only I see

One shot at this thing called life
Tens of ways to make things right
Hundreds of ways to be romantic
Thousands of ideas to show love
Millions of days to prove love
Billions of thoughts you will occupy

Tomorrow is never promised
Yesterday cannot be changed
Each hour is a mystery in life
Enjoy each minute you breath to the fullest
Never take for granted the chances you are given
Appreciate each opportunity you have
And do every action with love as the foundation

www.ingramcontent.com/pod-product-compliance
Lightning Source LLC
Chambersburg PA
CBHW060920130726
48001CB00006B/2337